Where will you be five years from today?

In loving memory of Bob Moawad

ACKNOWLEDGMENTS

The quotations in this book were gathered lovingly but unscientifically over several years and/or were contributed by many friends or acquaintances. Some arrived – and survived in our files – on scraps of paper and may therefore be imperfectly worded or attributed. To the authors, contributors and original sources, our thanks, and where appropriate, our apologies. ~The Editors

WITH SPECIAL THANKS TO

Jason Aldrich, Gerry Baird, Jay Baird, Neil Beaton, Josie Bissett, Laura Boro, Melissa Carlson, M.H. Clark, Tiffany Parente Connors, Jim & Alyssa Darragh & Family, Rob Estes, Pamela Farrington, Michael & Leianne Flynn & Family, Sarah Forster, Miriam Hathaway & Family, Michael Hedge, Liz Heinlein & Family, Renee & Brad Holmes, Jennifer Hurwitz, Heidi Jones, Sheila Kamuda, Michelle Kim, Carol Anne Kennedy, June Martin, David Miller, Carin Moore & Family, Moose, Jessica Phoenix & Tom DesLongchamp, Janet Potter & Family, Joanna Price, Heidi & Jose Rodriguez, Diane Roger, Alie Satterlee, Kirsten & Garrett Sessions, Andrea Summers, Brien Thompson, Helen Tsao, Anne Whiting, Heidi Yamada & Family, Justi and Tote Yamada & Family, Bob & Val Yamada, Kaz & Kristin Yamada & Family, Tai & Joy Yamada, Anne Zadra, August & Arline Zadra, and Gus & Rosie Zadra.

Credits

Written by Dan Zadra; Edited by Kristel Wills; Created by Kobi Yamada; Designed by Steve Potter

ISBN 978-1-932319-44-6

7th Printing.
Printed in China

You don't have to take life the way it comes to you. You can design your life to come to you the way you want it.

This is your life, your one-and-only-life, and you don't want to miss any part of it. So, what is it going to be? You decide. Starting today, you can make the next five years the most exciting, satisfying, productive and amazing years of your life so far—or just another five years.

The purpose of this book is to stir your creative juices and to inspire you to really get in touch with your dreams. The goal is not to provide a list of what "should" be done with the next five years—but to stir up some exciting possibilities of what "could" be done.

In the following pages, you'll find fresh ways of thinking about different areas of your life. It could be something as significant as tracing your roots, developing an exciting idea, pursuing a heart-quickening adventure, or finding creative ways to give back. The truth is, you really can turn any "what if?" into "what is."

Over the next five years, what do you really want to do? What do you really want to have? What do you really want to be? Where do you really want to go?

The future is sending back good wishes and waiting with open arms.
~Kobi Yamada

DECIDE
WHAT'S NEXT
IN YOUR LIFE
AND STRATEGIZE
HOW TO GET IT.

Five years...260 weeks...1,825 days...2,333,000 minutes.

What will you do with it? What *could* you do with it?

IN FIVE YEARS COLUMBUS OPENED UP A WHOLE NEW WORLD BY DISCOVERING THE BAHAMAS, CUBA, HISPANIOLA, AND NORTH AND SOUTH AMERICA.

IN JUST UNDER FIVE YEARS, MICHELANGELO PAINTED THE SISTINE CHAPEL.

IN LESS THAN FIVE YEARS SHAKESPEARE WROTE "HAMLET," "OTHELLO," "KING LEAR," "MACBETH" AND FIVE OTHER IMMORTAL PLAYS.

Don't say you don't have enough time. You have exactly the same number of hours per day that were given to Helen Keller, Louis Pasteur, Michelangelo, Mother Teresa, Leonardo da Vinci, Thomas Jefferson and Albert Einstein.

~H. Jackson Brown, Jr.

IN 1961, JULIA CHILD GRADUATED FROM COOKING SCHOOL WITH A QUIRKY IDEA FOR A TV SHOW. FOUR YEARS LATER SHE WON AN EMMY AS AMERICA'S FAVORITE TV CHEF.

FIRED FROM THEIR HOME IMPROVEMENT JOBS, ARTHUR BLANK AND BERNIE MARCUS CREATED A BUSINESS MODEL CALLED HOME DEPOT AND WENT PUBLIC WITH THEIR IDEA. JUST THREE YEARS AFTER LOSING THEIR JOBS, THEIR ANNUAL SALES WERE $1 BILLION.

AT AGE 30, AMAZON FOUNDER JEFF BEZOS WAS LIVING IN A 500-SQUARE FOOT APARTMENT. FIVE YEARS LATER HIS NET WORTH WAS $10 BILLION.

Live your life on purpose.

You have brains in your head and feet in your shoes
You can steer yourself any direction you choose.   ~Dr. Seuss
You're on your own and you know what you know
And you are the one who'll decide where to go.

The best day of your life is the day on which you decide your life is your own. No one to lean on, rely on or blame. The gift of life is yours, it is an amazing journey, and you alone are responsible for the quality of it. Life is about the choices you make—choose wisely. Start by choosing the two most important "guiding stars"—your values and your mission. Choose your values: Values are personal choices you make about what's important to you. Being guided by your highest values brings immense satisfaction and meaning to life. Examples of lifetime values: Family, Friendship, Health, Wealth, Learning, Sustainability, Career, Community, Faith, Integrity, Art, Free Time, Creativity, Adventure, Love.

Here are some questions that will help you identify
YOUR TOP VALUES IN LIFE.

WHAT ARE THE THREE THINGS I LIKE MOST AND LEAST ABOUT MYSELF?

WHO IS THE HAPPIEST PERSON I KNOW?

WHO ARE THE TWO PEOPLE I LIKE AND RESPECT THE MOST AND WHY?

WHO AM I?

MY TOP FIVE VALUES ARE:

Identifying your top five lifetime values is a shortcut to identifying your top goals in life.

1

2

3

4

5

CHOOSE YOUR MISSION

(Your life is worth a noble motive!)

Some examples of personal mission statements:

WALT DISNEY: My mission in life is to make people happy.

ERIC SCHMIDT, CEO, GOOGLE: My mission is to collect all the world's information and make it accessible to everyone.

ANITRA FREEMAN, ARTIST: I believe creativity is the essence of being human. I believe I make myself, and I won't buy my soul off the rack.

PHIL KNIGHT, FOUNDER, NIKE: My mission is to bring inspiration and innovation to every athlete in the world.

REBECCA JONES, RANCHER: My life's mission is to protect and save early American farm animals such as the American Guinea hog and the Ben Franklin turkey from extinction.

WRITE YOUR PERSONAL MISSION STATEMENT

Assignment: There's no specific format for writing your personal mission statement—only you will know how to write it—but try to keep it clear, brief and exciting. Just ask yourself, "What is my calling, my life's aim? What inspires me the most? What activity or service is my core values urging me to pursue?"

This may be the turning point your grandchildren will tell stories about years from now: the time you leap over the abyss to the other side of the Great Divide and begin your life in earnest. On the other hand, this moment of truth may end up being nothing more than a brief awakening when you glimpse what's possible on the other side of the Great Divide, but then tell yourself, "Nah, that's waaayyy too far to jump." In that case, your grandchildren will have to be content talking about what delicious cookies you used to bake or what your favorite sports team was. It will all depend on how brave you'll be.

~Rob Brezsny

Follow your dreams,

they know the way.

If you don't

have a dream,

how can you

Your imagination is the preview to life's coming attractions. ~ALBERT EINSTEIN

have a dream

come true?

A GOAL IS A DREAM SET TO PAPER. DON'T JUST THINK IT—INK IT!

According to Dave Kohl, professor emeritus at Virginia Tech., people who regularly write down their goals earn nine times as much over their lifetimes as the people who don't, and yet 80% of Americans say they don't have goals. Sixteen percent do have goals, but they don't write them down. Less than four percent write down their goals, and fewer than one percent actually review them on an ongoing basis. Guess which one percent?

WRITE YOUR DREAMS DOWN! (LOOK, THEY JUST BECAME GOALS!)

BALANCE IS BEAUTIFUL

Setting goals in only one or two areas of life is

like rowing a boat with only one oar—you go

round and round in only one direction. If you

use all your creativity in just one area of your

life, you are destined to be one-dimensional

in others. (What's the use of being a multi-

millionaire five years from now if you end up

with a broken family?)

On a scale of 1 to 7, where 1 means "not at all satisfied with my life" and 7 means "completely satisfied," the people on "Forbes" magazine's list of the 400 richest Americans average 5.8—the same as the Inuit people in Greenland and the cattle-herding Masai of Kenya, who live in dung huts with no electricity or running water. [from "Money Really Doesn't Buy Happiness," Whitley Strieber]

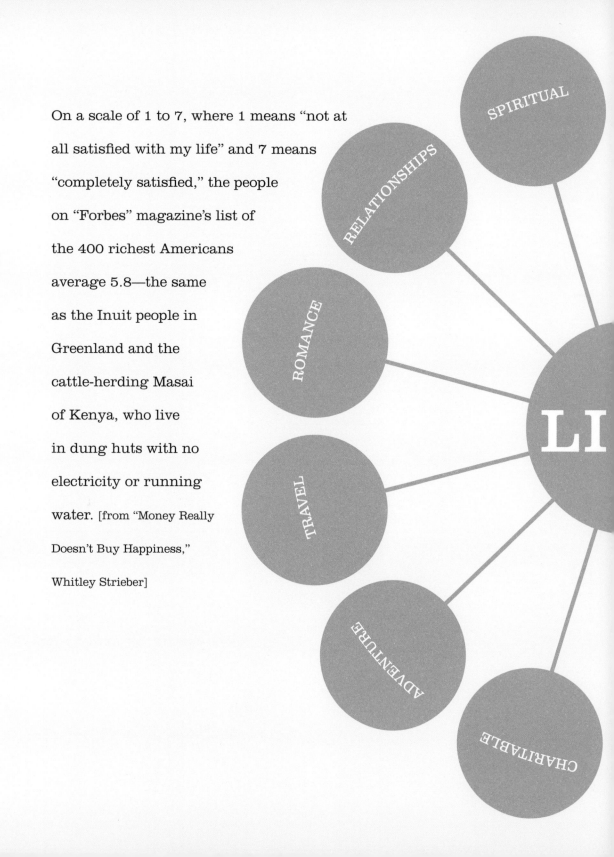

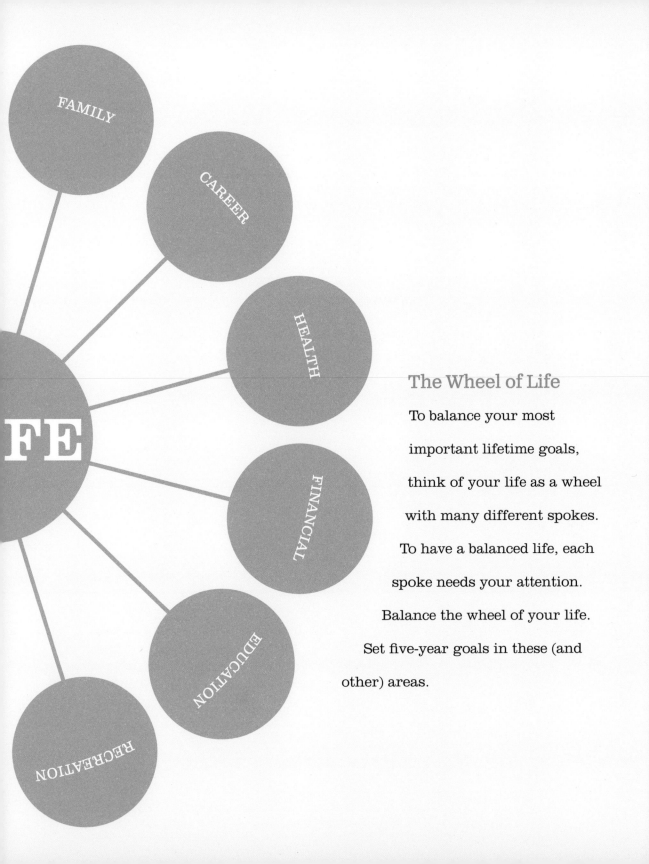

The Wheel of Life

To balance your most important lifetime goals, think of your life as a wheel with many different spokes. To have a balanced life, each spoke needs your attention. Balance the wheel of your life. Set five-year goals in these (and other) areas.

If you aim at nothing, you'll hit it every time.

~B.J. Marshall

When you walk into a restaurant, you don't just say, "Bring me some food."

Instead, you're very specific—you pick exactly what you want from the menu.

Do the same for your life. Don't just say, "My goal over the next five years is to

be happy." Be specific. The clearer and more vividly you visualize a goal, the

easier it becomes to achieve or acquire it. If possible, ride in it, fly in it,

visualize it, rehearse it, get pictures of it. Then list the steps needed to attain it.

Using vivid details, sketch or describe something you want, something that

will make you very happy—an experience, thing, place, goal or outcome.

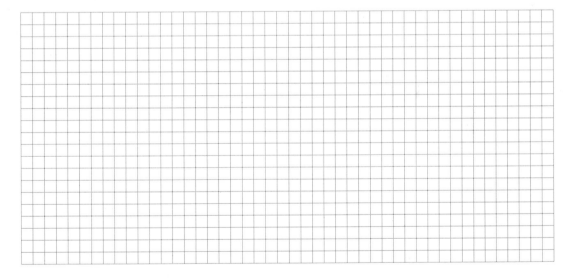

The tragedy of life does not lie in not reaching your goals, the tragedy lies in not having any

goals to reach. It isn't a calamity to die with dreams unfulfilled, but it is a calamity not to

dream. It is not a disaster to be unable to capture your ideals, but it is a disaster to have no

ideals to capture. It is not a disgrace not to reach the stars, but it is a disgrace to have no

stars to reach.   ~Dr. Benjamin Mays

Think

BIG

Most people **don't aim too high and miss. They aim too low and hit.**

~Bob Moawad

There isn't one person in a thousand who can write down his or her most exciting dreams without at the same time telling themselves that "it's probably impossible." The truth is, virtually anything is possible—nothing is too good to be true.

What would you attempt if you knew you could not fail? Write down a dream that you would love to pursue if you absolutely knew you could attain it. (It may be more doable than you think.)

Trading a Paper Clip for a House:

Thinking big, Kyle MacDonald started small—with a paperclip to be exact. He posted it on Craigslist as a barter and got a fish-shaped pen for it. He then traded the pen for something better. One trade led to another and another, until MacDonald finally found himself the new owner of a three-bedroom house.

Give yourself permission to aim high in work and life. Take time to dream and plan.

So many of our dreams at first seem impossible, then seem improbable, and then, when we summon the will, they soon seem inevitable. ~Christopher Reeve

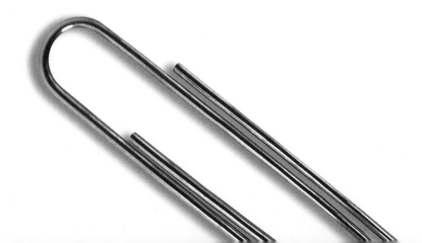

Chunk it!

Big ideas can be intimidating, but even your biggest and most daunting goal can be achieved if you simply break it up into bite-sized chunks. Struggling author Joseph Heller composed his best-selling book "Catch-22" by writing little chunks in one or two hours every day before work. Imagine what you could accomplish by applying the same principle to one or more of your biggest goals over the next five years. Remember: the sum total of a lot of little efforts isn't little.

Remember, also, to think for yourself. Who are "they" who exercise so much power over our lives? "They" said that Elvis Presley couldn't sing. "They" said that James Joyce couldn't write. "They" said that Michael Jordan couldn't play. What do "they" say about you?

Listen to the MUSTN'TS, child, listen to the DON'TS—listen to the SHOULDN'TS, the IMPOSSIBLES, the WON'TS—listen to the NEVER HAVES. Then listen close to me—anything can happen, child. ANYTHING can be. ~Shel Silverstein

Either you are living out someone else's dream for you, or you are setting your own course. Don't let other people tell you who you are. Form the habit of saying "Yes" to your own ideas. Then write down all the reasons why they will work. There will always be plenty of people around to tell you why they *won't* work.

To be nobody but yourself in a world which is doing its best day and night to make you like everybody else means to fight the hardest battle which any human being can fight—but never stop fighting! ~e.e. cummings

Surround yourself with people who believe you can.

By all means, share your goals— but only share them with people who can help you attain them.

Benchmark test for choosing friends: Will spending time with this person drag me down or lift me up? Will he or she make me want to be a better person? A happier person? A more successful person? Will he or she help me achieve my most important goals? If not, find some friends who will.

List five people who can help you achieve your dreams and goals.

One of my best moves is to surround myself with friends who, instead of asking, "Why?" are quick to say, "Why not?" That attitude is contagious.

~Oprah Winfrey

WHY NOT YOU? WHY NOT NOW?

Do it now!

Some people spend all their lives on a boring little island called the "Someday Isle." "Someday I'll be happy. Someday, I'll hike in Nepal. Someday I'll build a log house. Someday I'll have a great adventure." Life is not a dress rehearsal. Life is here and it is now. Reach out and seize it, you deserve it!

Assignment: List five things you've been procrastinating about and plan to take at least a little bit of action on all five this week. Do it now!

Each morning he'd stack up the letters he'd write...tomorrow. And think of the friends he'd fill with delight...tomorrow. It was too bad, indeed; he was busy today and hadn't a minute to stop on his way. "More time I'll give to others," he'd say...tomorrow. But the fact is he died and faded from view and all that he left when the living was through was a mountain of things he intended to do...tomorrow.

~Unknown

TGIM:

Dreading Mondays is a ridiculous way to spend one-seventh of your life, but that's the weird habit that millions of people have fallen into.

Imagine this: Over the next five years you'll receive the gift of 260 different Mondays, each one coming into your life fresh and full of promise. What kind of magic and miracles could you create with that kind of time? Why not be a maverick? Why not welcome every Monday with the same anticipation and excitement that most people reserve just for Fridays?

ASSIGNMENT: How could you put every Monday on a pedestal? What if you designated every Monday as Mom Day, or Friend Day, or Family Day, or Fun Day...or?

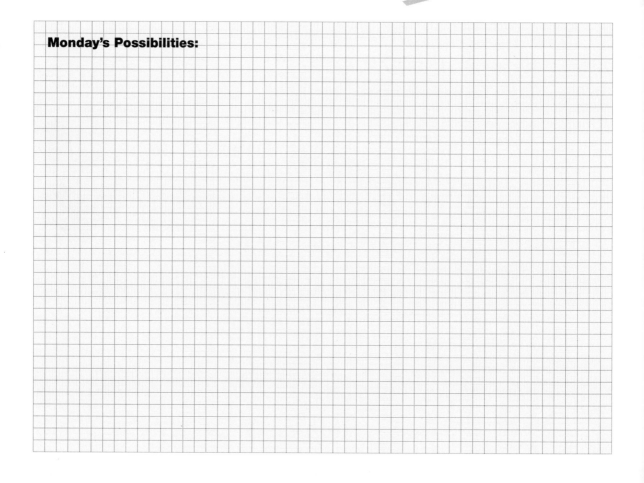

Monday's Possibilities:

God It's Monday!

S M T W T F S

1 2 3 4

6 7 8 9 10 11

13 14 15 16 17

20 21 22 23 2

27 28 29 30

DO YOU KNOW HOW AMA

ZING YOU TRULY ARE?

There has never been another you. You are a once-in-all-history event. You are new to nature. You are one of a kind; therefore, no one can really predict to what heights you might soar. Even you will not know until you spread your wings. You may not be able to see your undeveloped potential, but it's there—and it is enormous!

The Amazing You:

Your amazing instincts... Since the Ice Age, vast numbers of your ancestors have been smart enough, fast enough, strong enough and courageous enough to survive several thousand years of famine, plague, predators and the worst natural disasters. Though you may think of yourself as merely "average," you are actually the latest in a long line of human success stories...and the hidden strengths you've inherited are no doubt trying their best to emerge. Let them out!

The human mind is the fastest-working, coolest-running, most compact and efficient computer ever produced in large quantities by unskilled labor. ~Bob Moawad

Your amazing mind... The average human brain weighs about 2½ to 3 pounds. It is made up of about 30 billion cells called neurons. Each neuron is capable of handling approximately one million bits of information. The total number is so large, in fact, that if you sat down and wrote a number one, you would have to follow it with 6.5 million miles of zeros, a number that would stretch from the Earth to the moon and back more than 13 times.

Your amazing body... Your body has approximately 62,000 miles of capillaries; millions of electrical warning signals, railroad and conveyer systems; a fabulous built-in telephone system; and a highly sophisticated audio-visual system. You are a fantastic animal! A man can run a hundred yards in nine seconds. He can run for hours without stopping. He can leap almost 30 feet. He can climb a tree. He can swim—swiftly and far. The animals made for running may outrun us, the animals made for climbing may out-climb us, but there is no animal in the world that can do all of these as well as we can. ~James Dillet Freeman

Your amazing lifespan... Just 200 years ago the average American died by age 35. Today, we've more than doubled that number. Your chances of a longer, healthier life will continue to increase well into this century. What you are going to do with your longer, healthier life is an answer only you can give.

AN ELDERLY MAN, IN THE FINAL DAYS OF HIS LIFE, IS LYING IN BED ALONE. HE AWAKENS TO SEE A LARGE GROUP OF PEOPLE CLUSTERED AROUND HIS BED. THEIR FACES ARE LOVING, BUT SAD. CONFUSED, THE OLD MAN SMILES WEAKLY AND WHISPERS, "YOU MUST BE MY CHILDHOOD FRIENDS COME TO SAY GOOD-BYE. I AM SO GRATEFUL." MOVING CLOSER, THE TALLEST FIGURE GENTLY GRASPS THE OLD MAN'S HAND AND REPLIES, "YES, WE ARE YOUR BEST AND OLDEST FRIENDS, BUT LONG AGO YOU ABANDONED US. FOR WE ARE THE UNFUL-FILLED PROMISES OF YOUR YOUTH. WE ARE THE UNREALIZED HOPES, DREAMS AND PLANS THAT YOU ONCE FELT DEEPLY IN YOUR HEART, BUT NEVER PURSUED. WE ARE THE UNIQUE TALENTS THAT YOU NEVER REFINED, THE SPECIAL GIFTS THAT YOU NEVER DIS-COVERED. OLD FRIEND, WE HAVE NOT COME TO COMFORT YOU, BUT TO DIE WITH YOU."

From "I Believe in You"

WHAT WILL YOU DO
WITH YOUR TALENTS?

Talent is God's gift to you. What you do with it is your gift back. The things you are naturally good at are your gifts. If singing or dancing or math or music or leadership come easily to you, that's a gift. One of the marks of a gift is to have the courage to fulfill it. If it's easy for you to be a good dancer, or singer, or athlete, why not become a great one?

List some of your natural gifts and talents. Decide you'll become great at one or more over the next five years.

Life is truly a ride. We're all strapped in and no one can stop it. When the doctor slaps your behind, he's ripping your ticket and away you go. As you make each passage from youth to adulthood to maturity, sometimes you put your arms up and scream, sometimes you just hang onto that bar in front of you. But the ride is the thing. I think the most you can hope for at the end of life is that your hair is messed, you're out of breath and you didn't throw up.

~Unknown

Have ad

Take yourself by surprise.

Be unlike you now and then. ✦ Escape the treadmill of predictability. ✦ Wear colored socks. ✦ Take the scenic route to work. ✦ Re-tune your radio to Beethoven or Mariachi music for awhile. ✦ Feed the birds at lunch. ✦ Give blood or visit the food bank. ✦ Call your mother. ✦ Plant a flaming yellow rhododendron. ✦ Buy a vegetable or fruit you've never tried before. ✦ Write a love letter to your significant other. ✦ Turn off the TV and talk to your kids.

Break with routine

What happened to spontaneity? At what point did you lose the right to do something in your day just because you feel like it at the moment—just because you're alive?

ventures

Because of our routines we forget that life is an ongoing adventure.

~Maya Angelou

Do something brilliant every day.

Strike out in some new directions. ✦ Learn martial arts or creative dance. ✦ Make a spectacular presentation. ✦ Obliterate your sales goal. ✦ Dream a wonderful dream. ✦ Prepare an astounding meal. ✦ Tell an outrageous joke. ✦ Savor life. Remember, we only pass this way once.

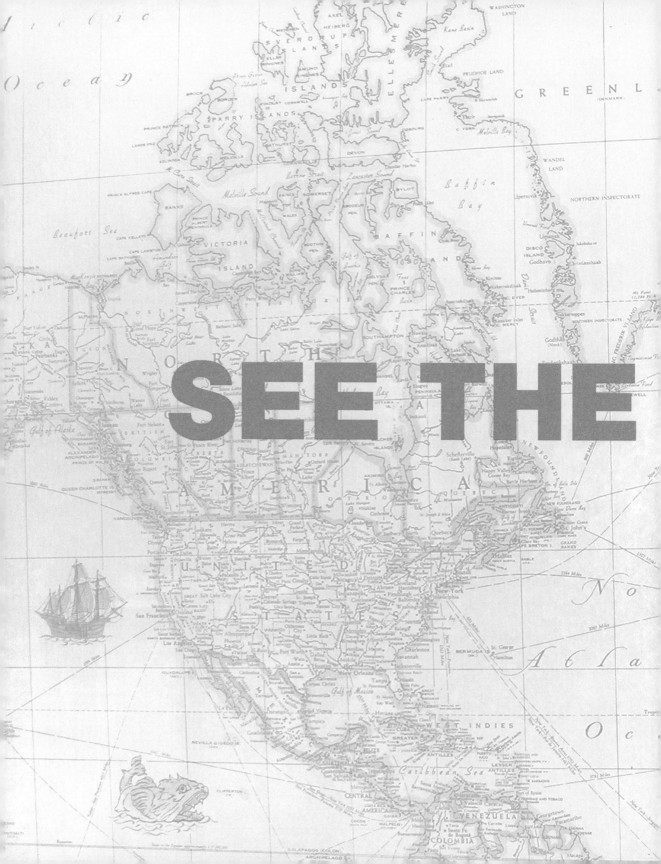

SEE THE

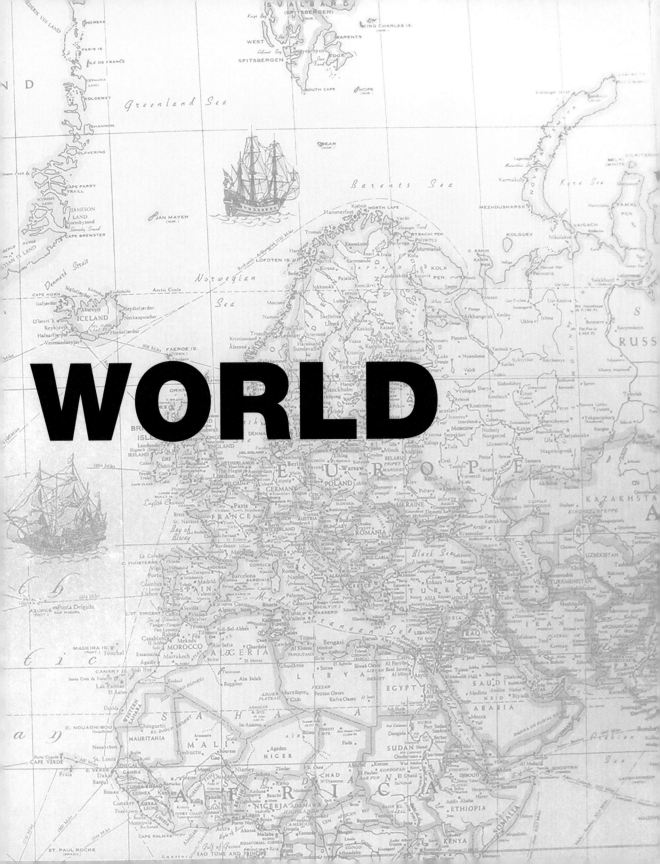

WORLD

wonder & wander

THE SEVEN NATURAL WONDERS
MOUNT EVEREST
THE GREAT BARRIER REEF
THE GRAND CANYON
VICTORIA FALLS
THE HARBOR OF RIO DE JANEIRO
PARICUTIN VOLCANO
THE NORTHERN LIGHTS

THE SEVEN MODERN WONDERS
THE EMPIRE STATE BUILDING
THE ITAIPÚ DAM
THE CN TOWER
THE PANAMA CANAL
THE CHANNEL TUNNEL
THE NORTH SEA PROTECTION WORKS
THE GOLDEN GATE BRIDGE

THE SEVEN FORGOTTEN NATURAL WONDERS
ANGEL FALLS
THE BAY OF FUNDY
IGUAÇÚ FALLS
KRAKATOA ISLAND
MOUNT FUJI
MOUNT KILIMANJARO
NIAGARA FALLS

THE SEVEN FORGOTTEN MODERN WONDERS
THE CLOCK TOWER (BIG BEN)
THE EIFFEL TOWER
THE GATEWAY ARCH
THE ASWAN HIGH DAM
HOOVER DAM
MOUNT RUSHMORE NATIONAL MEMORIAL
THE PETRONAS TOWERS

YOU SHALL SEE WONDERS! ~WILLIAM SHAKESPEARE

This is your life, your one-and-only-life—
shouldn't you see at least one Wonder for
yourself over the next five years?

Of the original seven wonders, only the
Great Pyramids at Giza are still intact.
But there are lots of other wonders to
choose from. Which will you see for yourself? Circle your top destinations or make
your own list, but go see them for yourself!

Who were your ancestors and how do you fit into their story? Were they lemon farmers in Amalfi, or olive merchants in Greece, or tradesmen in Africa, or Buddhist priests in Japan?

Visit the home of your ancestors.

Today, you can discover a lot about your ancestors in just 20 minutes and a few clicks of the mouse. Go online and type in the word "ancestry" and away you go.

Whoever your ancestors were, make plans to go see where they came from soon. Walk the hills or villages where they were born. Feel their dreams, hopes and aspirations. If possible, eat where they ate; drink where they drank; sing what they sang; sleep where they slept; pray where they prayed. You are the latest edition in a long line of your family. You deserve to see, hear, feel, taste and touch the home of your ancestors for yourself.

I ALWAYS WANTED TO...

SIT IN THE STANDS AT A WORLD CUP SOCCER GAME

STAND BEHIND THE TAPE ON THE 18TH HOLE AT THE MASTERS

WELCOME THE SWALLOWS AS THEY RETURN TO CAPISTRANO

FOLLOW THE MIGRATION OF THE MONARCH BUTTERFLIES

RUN WITH THE BULLS IN PAMPLONA, SPAIN

HAVE A PICNIC AT THE MONTEREY JAZZ FESTIVAL

FEEL THE OCEAN'S SPRAY AT THE AMERICA'S CUP RACE

BE PART OF THE EXCITEMENT AND GLORY OF THE OLYMPIC GAMES

CHEER FROM THE BLEACHERS AT A WORLD SERIES GAME

JOIN IN THE ODDITIES OF THE STAR TREK CONVENTION

RUN WILD AND BARTER MY SERVICES AT THE BURNING MAN FESTIVAL

Attend a world-class event.

I'm definitely going to...

Make a list of your own or select from the list above—but make it happen. Some things do not translate, you have to go to know.

Anousheh Ansari always loved looking up at the stars. So when she had the opportunity to become the first female space tourist, she jumped at the chance. After returning from space to the Cosmodome in Kazakhstan, Ansari said, "I loved being in space, and if I had a choice I would have probably stayed longer." Achieving her lifelong dream has only inspired her to keep dreaming of ways to get back up there.

TRUST YOUR CRAZY IDEAS

From the time we are in grade school, we're taught to think that the best answers and ideas are in books or come from someone else's head. What the world really needs to know right now is what kind of dreams and crazy new ideas are in *your* head!

It's easy to come up with big ideas. Just think of something that everyone agrees would be "wonderful" if it were only "possible"—and then set out to make it possible.
~Armand Hammer

In 2005 three college guys wished they had a simple way to share videos online with their friends. So they threw together a simple invention—a way for virtually any video to play on any web browser—and started their own little company called YouTube. One year later they sold their company to Google for $1.6 billion—and "Time" magazine named their idea "Invention of the Year."

What is *your* YouTube? Take out a notepad today

and write down some wonderful ideas to benefit

humanity. A single idea can transform a life, a

family, a business, a nation, a world. Most people

come up with one or two new ideas a year. Over

the next five years, dedicate yourself to having

one new idea every week. In five years, you'll

have 250 ideas—more than most people have

in a lifetime. Some of them will be pure genius.

Thousands of perceptions, hunches, ideas and intuitions race
through our brains every day. Some are pure genius. Give them the
red light for at least long enough to write them down. **~Ralph Ford**

Every day matters.

Live each day as if it's your last...because one day you'll be right.

Where are you on your journey?

1. Get out your pencil and
   do the math.

2. Multiply your age x 365
   days. *(That will give you
   your current age in days.)*

   $$
   \begin{array}{r}
   365 \\
   \text{x} \quad \text{your age} \\
   \text{in years} \\
   \hline
   = \\
   \end{array}
   $$

3. Subtract that number
   from 27,375 days.
   *(That's an average life-
   span (+/-) these days.)*

   $$
   \begin{array}{r}
   27,375 \\
   - \quad \text{your age} \\
   \text{in days} \\
   \hline
   = \\
   \end{array}
   $$

I probably have _____ days left.

LIFE IS TOO SHORT TO BE CRANKY

Attitude is a choice. We create our own world by the way we choose to see it. For the next five years your mind can focus on fear, worry, problems, negativity or despair. Or it can focus on confidence, opportunity, solutions, optimism and success. You decide.

KEEP YOUR WORD

Say what you mean, and mean what you say. Look the world straight in the eye. Live and work with honesty, openness and integrity; keep your promises, and everything else is a piece of cake.

FORGIVE EVERYONE, ESPECIALLY YOURSELF

Let go of past hurts. Feelings of resentment (or revenge) are worthless—they can only drag you down. The courage to forgive and move on is so liberating. Make it a rule: "Always be the first to forgive—especially yourself."

MOVE FORWARD

Yesterday is a cancelled check. The past is not your potential. There are far better things ahead than any you leave behind. The next five years are a blank canvas—clean and bright. Decide that you will throw all the paint on it you can.

QUIT WORRYING

It's been estimated that 99 out of 100 things we worry about never come to pass. If you stopped worrying about what might happen tomorrow, wouldn't that give you more time to actually enjoy and savor today? What did you worry about six months ago? A year ago? Five years ago? How many of your biggest worries have actually come to pass?

BE GRATEFUL

Stop and view your life through the eyes of the other six billion people on Earth. Literally hundreds of millions of people would gladly trade places with you right now—and be ecstatic.

IT'S THE LITTLE THINGS

Thinking small is an art—the art of living. The happiness of life is made up of little things—a smile, a helping hand, a caring heart, a word of praise, a moment of shared laughter. We are most alive in those moments. Savor them all!

What you focus on increases.

Faced with a significant problem or setback, many people simply give up on their dreams or plans. Instead, try treating problems as opportunities to be creative. Realize that for every obstacle there is a solution. Discover the magic of searching for the "second right answer."

LOOK FOR THE SECOND RIGHT ANSWER

Here's an example: Suppose you and your significant other have been planning to quit work and spend the next few years exploring the highways and byways of America in your shiny new Winnebago. **Here's the problem:** Now that you're finally ready to head off into the sunset, you realize that the price of gas has skyrocketed, and you haven't saved nearly as much money as you need. What would you do—give up? **Here's a second right answer:** When faced with a similar situation, Daniel Ford, 57, and his wife Becky, 51, looked for the opportunity in their problem and found it: Instead of buying an RV and paying for all that gas, insurance and upkeep, the Ford's applied for a job as a long-haul truck driving couple. Instead of traveling America in a Winnebago, they hit the road in a fully-equipped 18-wheeler. Instead of tapping their savings as they had originally planned, they were actually paid to see the country. **Here's the principle:** Always look closely for the second right answer. What, at first, appears to be a broken dream may actually be a dream come true.

Your resources are always far greater than you imagine them to be.
Never ask, "Can I do this?" Ask instead, "How can I do this?" ~Dan Zadra

Celebrate those who helped you.

Somebody saw something in you once—and that is partly why you're where you are today. An inspiring teacher, a loving parent, a caring friend, an encouraging coach, a thoughtful co-worker. Whoever helped you along the way, find a way to thank them.

Over the next five years, go back over your life and take time to thank the people who made a difference for you along the way. A note, call or visit from you—out of the blue—will mean the world to them. Thank them not just for what they have done for you, but for what they mean to you.

Start your "thank you" list on the next page today.

If you can read this, thank a teacher.

~NY Library System

A childhood playmate. Your first best friend. A cherished teacher. An inspiring coach or 4-H leader. A thoughtful neighbor. Your college roommate. Your best man or maid of honor. The rabbi or minister who tied the knot. The physician who delivered your baby. A caring mentor. Or just a friend or family member who gave you the support you needed to get where you are today.

People I am

grateful for:

If you have something to say to a
loved one, don't wait until tomorrow.
Too late comes sooner than later.

~Nick Welton

When was the last time

you did
something
for the
first time?

Don't "go" through life —"grow" through life.

Realize that the journey of life is not about being right or pretending that you know it all—it's about learning and growing every step of the way.

Instead of getting stuck in a rut, or holding yourself back, make your life an adventure. Decide today that your commitment to learning and growing over the next five years is bigger than your commitment to staying the same.

I would rather be ashes than dust; I would rather that my spark should burn out in a brilliant blaze than it should be stifled by dry-rot; I would rather be in a superb meteor, every atom of me in a magnificent glow than in a sleepy and permanent planet; the proper function of man is to live, not to exist; I shall not waste my days in trying to prolong them; I shall USE my time.

~Jack London

READ THE GREAT BOOKS: PICK UP HOMER'S "ILIAD" AND PREPARE TO BE AMAZED. SEE THE FACE THAT LAUNCHED A THOUSAND SHIPS, HEAR THE ANCIENT CLASH OF SHIELDS AND THE CALL OF TROJAN TRUMPETS FOR YOURSELF. BUT DON'T STOP THERE. READ LEONARDO DA VINCI'S "NOTEBOOKS," OR CERVANTES' "DON QUIXOTE," OR TOLSTOY'S "WAR AND PEACE," OR JANE AUSTEN'S "PRIDE AND PREJUDICE," OR HERMAN MELVILLE'S "MOBY DICK" AND YOU'LL NEVER BE THE SAME AGAIN. *ONE GLANCE AT A BOOK AND YOU ACTUALLY HEAR THE VOICE OF ANOTHER PERSON, PERHAPS SOMEONE DEAD FOR 1,000 YEARS. TO READ IS TO VOYAGE THROUGH TIME. ~CARL SAGAN* **LEARN ANOTHER LANGUAGE:** LEARNING A SECOND LANGUAGE IS A NEW WAY TO SEE AND EXPERIENCE THE WORLD. LEARN ITALIAN, RUSSIAN, COBAL, AMERICAN SIGN LANGUAGE, FARSI OR SWAHILI. THEN GET ON A PLANE AND GO TRY IT OUT WITH THE PEOPLE WHO KNOW IT BEST. **MASTER A SKILL:** DON'T JUST BE GOOD, BE GREAT. TAKE AN "INTEREST" AND ELEVATE IT INTO AN ART FORM. LEARN TO DO SOMETHING SO WELL THAT PEOPLE WILL COME FROM MILES AROUND JUST TO WATCH YOU DO IT AGAIN AND AGAIN. **BECOME A MASTER:** SCRABBLE PLAYER, MAGICIAN, FRENCH CHEF, VENTRILOQUIST, BALLROOM DANCER, WINE MAKER, ORCHID GROWER, GLASS BLOWER, MARTIAL ARTIST, FRISBEE CHAMP, PHOTOGRAPHER, STANDUP COMEDIAN. **KICK A HABIT:** IF THERE IS ANYTHING IN YOUR LIFE THAT IS HOLDING YOU BACK, NOW IS THE TIME TO THINK ABOUT CHANGING IT. WHAT HABITS ARE CURRENTLY PREVENTING THE BEST THAT IS IN YOU? (ON AVERAGE, IT TAKES ABOUT 30 DAYS TO CHANGE A NEGATIVE HABIT INTO A POSITIVE HABIT—BUT THE BENEFITS WILL LAST A LIFETIME!) **TRANSFORM NEGATIVES:** WHAT BUGS YOU? A FAST TRACK TO HAPPINESS AND FULFILLMENT IS TO ZERO IN ON WHATEVER MAKES YOU UNHAPPY, AND TURN THOSE NEGATIVES INTO POSITIVES. IDENTIFYING WHAT BUGS YOU ABOUT YOURSELF OR YOUR LIFE IS A LESSON IN INSTANT CLARITY. **GET FIT:** YOGA, RUNNING, ROCK CLIMBING, HULA HOOP—IT DOESN'T MATTER WHAT YOU DO, BUT DO IT. GET IN THE BEST SHAPE OF YOUR LIFE. OVER THE NEXT FIVE YEARS YOU CAN HAVE THE BODY, THE ENERGY AND THE HEALTH YOU'VE ALWAYS WANTED.

lifeis

It's never too late

or too early.

Right now is a good time.

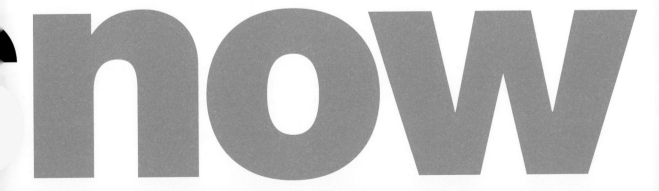

Forget your age. Clearly it's what you do—not when you do it—that really counts.

At age 7 Mozart wrote his first symphony.

At 14 country singer LeAnn Rimes won her first two Grammy awards.

At 16 swimmer Shane Gould won three Olympic Gold medals.

At 17 Joan of Arc led an Army in defense of France.

At 20 Debbi Fields founded Mrs. Fields cookie company.

At 21 Fred DeLuca co-founded Subway with just $1,000 in the bank.

At 43 John F. Kennedy ran for the U.S. Presidency, and won.

At 45 boxer George Foreman regained the heavyweight championship of the world.

At 46 Jack Nicklaus won his sixth Masters tournament.

At 54 jockey Willie Shoemaker won the Kentucky Derby.

At 57 Ray Kroc founded MacDonald's.

At 62 Colonel Sanders devoted himself to Kentucky Fried Chicken.

At 78 Grandma Moses started painting and was still participating in one-woman art shows well into her nineties.

At 83 architect Frank Lloyd Wright was asked which of his masterpieces was the best. "My next one," he said.

At 84 Titian painted his famous "Allegory of the Battle of Lepanto."

At 86 Ruth Rothfarb ran the Boston Marathon in just over five hours. "You lose a lot of speed between 80 and 86," she joked.

On his 104th birthday Cal Evans was interviewed by a Denver reporter. "Have you lived in Denver all your life?" asked the reporter. Cal laughed and replied, "Not yet, Sonny."

Here is the test to determine whether your mission on earth is finished: If you're alive, it isn't.

~Richard Bach

Whether you're five or 105, you have a lifetime ahead of you—so renew your dreams! What are you passionate about? What is something you've always wanted to do but haven't done? Right now is a good time.

_____

_____

_____

_____

_____

Never retire! Do what you do and keep doing it. But don't do it on Friday. Take Friday off. Friday, Saturday, and Sunday, go fishing... Then from Monday to Thursday, do what you've been doing all your life. My point is:
Live fully and don't retreat.

~Mel Brooks

You are the hero of your own story.

Be the answer to someone's prayers.

Dr. Jo Blessing tells the story of a chance meeting between two strangers. An older woman had been sitting on a park bench, despondent and lonely, thinking of suicide, when a young man sat down next to her. The two of them fed the pigeons together for a few minutes. Finally the young man got up, turned to the woman and thanked her for such a nice time. This seemingly small kindness restored the woman's faith in life. The young man never knew that he had been the answer to her prayers.

On any given day, without really realizing it, you may be the answer to someone's prayers. If you're too busy to reach out to people in your neighborhood or community, you're too busy. Never forget that your touch, your thoughtfulness and your love really can work wonders in the lives of others.

We are here on earth to do good for others. What the others are here for I do not know.

~W. H. Auden

Once a week over the next five years call someone you care about. Call a lonely neighbor, or visit an elderly person in a retirement community. Take a walk. Enjoy the sun together. Eat a Popsicle. Laugh, hug, cry or feed the birds together.

To the world you may be just one person, but to one person you may be the world.

~Josephine Billings

HOW WILL YOU

CHANGE THE WORLD?

I get up every morning determined both to
change the world and to have one hell of a good time.
Sometimes this makes planning the day difficult.

~E.B. White

Muhammad Yunus dreamed of "bringing dignity to the hundreds of millions of people all around the world who struggle every day to make a living and bring hope for a better life for their children." He started by making a small "micro loan" to some impoverished bamboo weavers. They needed to buy some weaving tools, and they didn't want to turn to loan sharks. They had no credit, but that didn't stop Yunus and his big idea: loaning business development money to the less fortunate. The weavers thrived, and for his pioneering concept of microcredit, Yunus won the Nobel Peace Prize. Overall, he's lent $5.7 billion to about 7 million people, many of them living in remote villages of the world. With the money from the award, he hopes to put "homelessness and destitution in a museum."

You are the one you've been waiting for.
Write down your ideas and go make the world better.

You don't have to quit your job or sacrifice your family or all your free time to make a difference in the world. One person like you can change the social landscape of our country in a few hours a week.

How? "If every American donated five hours a week," writes Whoopi Goldberg, "it would equal the labor of twenty million full-time volunteers."

May God bless you with tears to shed for those who suffer from pain, rejection, starvation and war, so that you will reach out your hand to comfort them and change their pain into joy. And may God bless you with the foolishness to think that you can make a difference in the world, so that you will do the things which others tell you cannot be done.

~A Franciscan Benediction

What do you care about? If you think somebody should do something about it, be somebody. Make a list of causes you are passionate about, then get involved.

volunteer

IF YOU ARE SUCCESS-

FUL IN ANY AREA OF **LIFE**, REMEMBER

THAT SOMEWHERE, SOMETIME, **SOMEONE** GAVE YOU

A LIFT OR AN IDEA THAT STARTED YOU IN THE RIGHT DIRECTION.

EACH OF US CAN **LOOK BACK** ON SOMEONE WHOSE SIMPLE **ACTS** OF

CARING CHANGED OUR LIVES—NOT JUST BY TEACHING US, BUT BY **TAKING**

THE TIME TO BE WITH US AND TO **BELIEVE IN US. DECIDE TODAY** THAT YOU

WILL MAKE TIME IN YOUR **LIFE** TO **MENTOR** SOMEONE—THAT YOU WILL **GIVE**

M E N T O R   S O M E O N E

THEM THE GIFT THAT ONLY YOU CAN GIVE. DON'T JUST GIVE WHAT YOU KNOW,

GIVE **WHO YOU ARE**. CAN'T THINK OF SOMEONE TO MENTOR? **DON'T**

LET THAT STOP YOU. **WHY NOT** BECOME A BIG PERSON TO A LITTLE

PERSON. JUST CONTACT **BIG BROTHERS** OR **BIG SISTERS**.

THEY'LL SHOW YOU HOW "BIGS" AND "LITTLES" ARE

MATCHED UP TO CREATE MEMORIES THAT

LAST A LIFETIME.

THANK YOU FOR BELIEVING IN ME BEFORE I BELIEVED IN MYSELF.

~KOBI YAMADA

How do **you** want to be remembered?

The following quiz appeared on the web and has been all over the world. See how you do:

1. Name the five wealthiest people in the world.
2. Name the last five Heisman Trophy winners.
3. Name the last five winners of the Miss America contest.
4. Name ten people who have won the Nobel or Pulitzer Prize.
5. Name the last half dozen Academy Award winners for best actor and actress.
6. Name the last decade's worth of World Series winners.

The point: None of us remember the headliners of yesterday. These are not second-rate achievers. They are the best in their fields. But the applause dies. Awards tarnish. Achievements are forgotten. Accolades and certificates are buried with their owners.

Here's another quiz. See how you do on this one:

1. List a few teachers who aided your journey through school.
2. Name three friends who have helped you through a difficult time.
3. Name three people who have taught you something worthwhile.
4. Think of a few people who have made you feel appreciated and special.
5. Think of three people you enjoy spending time with.
6. Name half a dozen heroes whose stories have inspired you.

Easier?

The lesson: The people who make a difference in your life are not the ones with the most credentials, the most money or the most awards. They are the ones who care.

~Unknown

DEFINE YOUR OWN SUCCESS

Success is the progressive realization of a worthy ideal.
~Earl Nightingale

Success is the side-effect of your personal dedication to a course greater than yourself.
~Viktor Frankl

Success is relishing life and doing whatever makes you truly happy.
~Vince Pfaff

Success is living up to your potential. Don't just show up for life—live it, enjoy it, taste it, smell it, feel it.
~Joe Kapp

Success? Odd as it seems, you will achieve the greatest results in business and career if you drop the word "achievement" from your vocabulary and replace it with "contribution."
~Peter Drucker

Success is not counted by how high you have climbed but by how many people you brought with you.
~Wil Rose

Write down your definition of success.

If success is not on your terms—if it looks good to the world but does not feel good in your own heart—it is no success at all.
~Anna Quindlen

When you reach the end of your life do you want to be one of the people who are glad they did, or one of the people who wish they had? Start doing the things today that will matter tomorrow. Don't leave this world without giving it your all. The best inheritance you can leave your kids is an example of how to live a full and meaningful life. Live your life so that your children can tell their children that you not only stood for something wonderful—you acted on it! *~Dan Zadra*

CLOSE YOUR EYES
FOR A FEW MINUTES
AND IMAGINE THAT
TODAY IS YOUR 100TH
BIRTHDAY. YOUR
CHILDREN AND
GRANDCHILDREN
ARE THROWING
A PARTY—AND
A NEWSPAPER
REPORTER HAS
COME TO
INTERVIEW YOU.

WHAT DO YOU
WANT TO TELL THE
REPORTER ABOUT
YOUR LIFE? YOUR
ACCOMPLISHMENTS?
YOUR REGRETS?
NOW, OPEN YOUR
EYES. IT'S NOT
TOO LATE—YOU
HAVE A FRESH
START ON LIFE!

"I don't want to get to the end of my life and find that I lived just the length of it. I want to have lived the width of it as well."

~Diane Ackerman

THIS IS A RECORD OF YOUR TIME. THIS IS YOUR MOVIE. LIVE OUT YOUR DREAMS

AND FANTASIES. WHISPER QUESTIONS TO THE SPHINX AT NIGHT. SIT FOR HOURS

AT SIDEWALK CAFES AND DRINK WITH YOUR HEROES. MAKE PILGRIMAGES TO

MOUGINS AND ABIQUIU. LOOK UP AND DOWN. BELIEVE IN THE UNKNOWN FOR IT

IS THERE. LIVE IN MANY PLACES. LIVE WITH FLOWERS AND MUSIC AND BOOKS AND

PAINTINGS AND SCULPTURE. KEEP A RECORD OF YOUR TIME. LEARN TO READ

WELL. LEARN TO LISTEN AND SPEAK WELL. KNOW YOUR COUNTRY, KNOW YOUR

WORLD, KNOW YOUR HISTORY, KNOW YOURSELF. TAKE CARE OF YOURSELF

PHYSICALLY AND MENTALLY. YOU OWE IT TO YOURSELF. BE GOOD TO THOSE AROUND

YOU. AND DO ALL OF THESE THINGS WITH PASSION. GIVE ALL THAT YOU CAN.

REMEMBER, LIFE IS SHORT AND DEATH IS LONG. ~FRITZ SHOULDER

You will never have more time than you do right now.